Unlock Your Creativity

A 21-day sensory workout for writers

Unlock Your Creativity

A 21-day sensory workout for writers

Sue Johnson and Val Andrews

**COMPASS
BOOKS**

Winchester, UK
Washington, USA

First published by Compass Books, 2014
Compass Books is an imprint of John Hunt Publishing Ltd., Laurel House, Station Approach,
Alresford, Hants, SO24 9JH, UK
office1@jhpbooks.net
www.johnhuntpublishing.com
www.compass-books.net

For distributor details and how to order please visit the 'Ordering' section on our website.

Text copyright: Sue Johnson and Val Andrews, 2013

ISBN: 978 1 78279 302 1

A CIP catalogue record for this book is available from the British Library.

Design: Lee Nash

Printed and bound by CPI Group (UK) Ltd, Croydon, CR0 4YY

We operate a distinctive and ethical publishing philosophy in all
areas of our business, from our global network of authors to
production and worldwide distribution.

CONTENTS

This book is dedicated to anyone who has pushed through self doubt, time constraints, financial restrictions and the negative influences of others, to make their creative wishes become a reality.

Introduction

We are all born creative. If you think back to when you were a child, the world was a magical place and it seemed like anything was possible. Then you got older, went to school and began to discover, if you hadn't already, that there were 'rules' and your days were mapped out for you. You were told off for daydreaming and looking out of the window – times when you probably travelled to that magical space 'beyond'. You had homework to do and your free time was taken up with after school clubs and other activities. Your work was marked 'right' or 'wrong' in red ink.

By the time you started work or college it is possible that your creative spark was buried under an avalanche of daily chores. The doorway to those pathways inside the head that led to stories, songs and paintings had become blocked and you told yourself and other people that you have no imagination.

"Don't waste your time," we've heard well-meaning friends say when somebody takes their first steps towards a new creative venture. If the person fails to produce an artistic masterpiece or a Booker prize winning novel within the first term, this can then lead to a loss of confidence, particularly if it is added to any negative messages from childhood.

It is never too late to reclaim your creative pathway and achieve your dreams. If you had creative ideas and a talent for writing and drawing when you were younger, this will still be there somewhere. By working through the exercises in the book, you will gradually find your way back to the doorway that leads to creative adventures and rediscover the pathway you are meant to follow. If you feel you should be living more creatively, then buying this book could be your first step towards achieving that goal.

We began running our 'Unlock Your Creativity' workshops as

a way of helping and encouraging people to release their creative blockages and take their first steps towards their dreams. Working with a variety of artistic and holistic techniques – collage, meditation, music and aromatherapy – we have seen so many people grow in confidence in a short space of time. We have written this book as a way of sharing with a larger number of people the ideas we have used and developed. The ideas and exercises in this book are intended for use whenever you feel in need of a creative boost.

It takes 21 days to change a habit or develop a new one, so this book is in easy to follow sections so that you can easily add creative sparkle to your life and begin to work towards your goals. You are never too young or too old to reclaim your creative pathway and succeed as a writer.

If you would like to rediscover your imaginative pathways, live a richer life without becoming financially poorer and achieve your ambitions as a writer, then this book is for you.

Who would find this book helpful?

We all need a creative boost sometimes. Working as a writer – whether full or part time – requires a lot of physical, mental and emotional energy. It is important that you take care of yourself and replenish that depleted energy on a regular basis. Failure to do so can result in writer's block or creative burn-out. The exercises in 'Unlock Your Creativity' will help any writer who recognises the value of refilling that creative well on a regular basis.

If you are temporarily blocked on a project, then by taking a few days to follow the exercises in 'Unlock Your Creativity' you should find that the words are soon flowing again. You can return to the book as many times as you wish to or build some of the exercises into your daily writing routine.

Young writers who have just completed a Creative Writing degree will find this is a useful introduction to how to actually 'be' a writer. By following the exercises regularly, you will have a structure to your days and will develop good habits of self nurturing and regular writing from the start.

Anyone suffering from personal trauma or creative breakdown – possibly following divorce or serious illness – will find the exercises in 'Unlock Your Creativity' useful for getting themselves back on track and moving on with their lives. Writing has been shown to be therapeutic in these situations. This book provides a structure for people to follow in addition to simple exercises that are fun to do and that produce results.

Creative writing tutors will find this book useful when planning their workshop exercises. 'Unlock Your Creativity' contains a variety of tried and tested ideas and techniques.

Begin your journey now – and don't forget to reward yourself every step of the way.

About us

Sue Johnson is published as a poet, short story writer and novelist. Her novel 'Fable's Fortune' is published by Indigo Dreams Publishing. 'The Yellow Silk Dress' – a novel set in London, Cornwall and Paris will be published by them in 2013. She has published two non-fiction books 'Creative Alchemy: 12 steps from inspiration to finished novel' (HotHive Books 2011) and 'Surfing the Rainbow: visualization and chakra balancing for writers' (Compass Books 2013). Sue's interests include reading, yoga and music. She is a Writers' News Home Study tutor and runs her own brand of writing classes. Her website address is www.writers-toolkit.co.uk. She and Val Andrews launched their successful 'Unlock Your Creativity' workshops in 2012.

Val Andrews is a visual artist and creative writer. She has designed an extensive range of fabrics and has self published a number of photo journals of her travels through Europe and England. Val has recently finished her first novel '12 weeks: journey of an escape artist' based on her travels through France and Spain, and is currently working on a novel for children, titled 'Rupert's Garden'. In her spare time she is also a painter and printmaker. She is passionately interested in the creative process, and helping others to unlock their own creative potential.

Part One
About You

Some questions to consider

Please take a moment to reflect on the questions below. Jot down your answers on a piece of paper, or better still, buy a really nice journal or notebook; something that is special to you, that you will enjoy touching, opening and writing in.

- How often do you write?
- How much does getting published matter to you?
- Why do you want this?
- What are you prepared to give up?
- How persistent are you?
- What difference will creative success make to your life?
- Who else could benefit from your success?

Focusing your intentions

For this first section you will need at least two hours of uninterrupted time so that you can focus on opening up to your creativity.

You will need:

- Pen
- Paper
- Large sheet of art paper – A3 size seems to work best for many people.
- Old magazines or photographs – anything that grabs your eye.
- Scissors
- Glue
- Felt tips or crayons
- Mandala pattern – there are numerous books on mandalas, so we've listed a few in at the end of this book. For getting you started quickly and cheaply, we recommend you go to Google Images and type in 'free mandala colouring patterns for adults' and see what you get. New designs are being added all the time.

Actions

Make a list of your writing wishes, as if money and time were no barriers. Write down everything you can think of, even if some of them feel a bit scary at the moment. You will grow into them!

- Where are you now with your writing?
- Where would you like to be in five years time? What will your life be like?
- What will the 'new you' look and behave like?
- Identify anything that is holding you back. Many people talk about negative messages from the past, like a teacher they didn't get on with or a disapproving parent. Your blockage may be related to a past relationship or something in the present. What is it? Write it down in detail.
- Pick one writing wish that you can make a start on now.

Visualisation for success

There are many guided visualisations available for free from the internet. For a guided meditation with a voice, you will find several to choose from. Just go to 'Google' then select 'You Tube' and type 'guided meditation' or 'guided meditation for creativity' or 'creative visualisation'.

You may prefer to read a meditation script out loud onto a small sound recording device, or have a trusted friend read it to you. We especially like the ones listed on the 'Inner Health Studio' website, so we've provided their web address at the end of this book. Here's one of their visual meditations which we've modified for you:

Begin by finding a quiet place in which you can relax without any interruptions. Find a comfortable position. If possible, take off your shoes. For the next few moments, focus on your breathing.

In... out...
In... out...

Continue to breathe slowly and peacefully as you allow the tension to leave your body. Release the areas of tension, feeling your muscles relax, becoming more comfortable with each breath. Continue to let your breathing relax you....

Breathe in...2...3...4... hold...2...3... out...2...3...4...5
Breathe in again...2...3...4...hold...2...3...out...2...3...4...5

Continue to breathe slowly, gently, comfortably. Let your breathing become slower as your body relaxes. Picture in your mind a place where you can completely relax. Imagine what this place looks like, sounds like and feels like. Make it a place in which you feel calm, safe and deeply relaxed.

- Notice the details of this special place:
- Are you alone here, or is someone with you?
- Are there any animals or birds?
- Is there water?
- Do you hear the sounds of nature or music, or just silence?
- What colours do you see?
- Is there any particular scent in this place?
- What is the temperature like?
- Is there a breeze or is it still?
- Remember that everything you sense is created by you. This is your place; a place which you are in control of, a place in which you feel safe, calm and deeply relaxed.
- Notice what you want to do here:
- Do you just sit still and soak in the surroundings?
- Do you get up and explore?
- Do you have any questions you would like to ask?
- Enjoy being here for as long as you need to.

Ask yourself

- What do you want to remember about this place?
- Where in this place will you choose to enter again at a later time?
- What do you want to take away from here?
- What do you want to leave behind?
- Slowly bring your attention back to the present moment. Feel your body on the chair or floor upon which you are actually resting now.
- Stretch your fingers and toes. Stretch your legs and arms. Roll your shoulders up and around behind you.
- Take two or three deep energising breaths and exhale fully. Slowly open your eyes.
- Take a few moments to readjust and make sure that you feel grounded. Imagine your feet as tree roots pushing into the earth.
- It is a good idea to eat or drink something before going on with your day.

Now write about what you saw as fully as you can, using all the senses

- Describe the details of this special place;
- Explain in detail what you wanted to do there;
- Explain what you wanted to leave and take away from this place and why; and
- Notice yourself as the person in this place, in particular:
- What colour outfit were you wearing?
- What sort of fabric was it made of?
- How did you feel about the things you heard, saw, smelled and felt?
- Did you eat or drink anything?

Answer these questions on your piece of paper

- What is different from your usual environment?
- What do you need in your life to become the person you want to be?
- What do you need to give up?
- What do you need to receive?
- Are there any practical barriers in your life that you need to deal with to fully open to your creative self?
- What can you do about this?

Affirmation

An affirmation could be described as a statement of purpose or intent. It's a great way of reminding yourself of what is important to you, and it acts by keeping you continuously focused on your creative goals.

The best place to start is to reflect on what you got from your visual meditation exercise, and then state what you want. Identify what's blocking you from getting what you want. For instance, you may be remembering a negative comment from another person or a negative experience in the past that has dampened your creative confidence. Recall this in detail and then re-write it. For example, you may previously have been told that you're lazy, or lacking in talent. If so, your positive affirmation would be 'I am hard-working and successful.'

Other examples:

"I finish what I start."
"I am bursting with creative ideas."
"I am a successful and published writer."

Choose an affirmation that will support you in achieving your creative goals. Don't worry if it doesn't fit your current image of yourself, because you will grow into it! Write it on several pieces of paper or card and keep them where you can see them often – e.g. in your pocket or handbag, by your bed, by your writing space.

Mandala

A mandala is a pattern, usually in a circular shape that can be used to help focus the mind on a particular plan or goal. It was originally developed by Buddhist and Hindu religions, as early as 4BC. It was a sacred art form, and used as an aid to meditation. The famous psychoanalyst Carl Jung (1875-1961) believed the mandala represents the subconscious desires of the person creating it; hence its use nowadays as a tool for focusing the mind on goals.

How to do it – Go to 'Google', select 'Images' and type 'free mandala colouring patterns for adults' into the search bar. You will see a great variety of mandala designs. Choose one that really appeals to you and print it – or create your own.

Colour in the patterns with as many different colours as you wish. Focus on colouring within the lines, all the while reflecting on your affirmation and your creative goals. Write your affirmation on, above or around your mandala; whichever composition is most appealing to you.

Collage for success

Go through some old magazines and tear out pictures and words that support your future vision of yourself. These could be a bottle of champagne, the word 'star', a picture of the outfit you might wear to an awards ceremony or book signing, a place you would like to visit, a huge box of chocolates – the list is endless!

Have fun choosing what you would like to include in your collage. Don't think too deeply about it, just go for it. Position the images onto your paper. When you are happy with the composition, glue them down. Place your mandala somewhere on, around or near the collage and then pin it where you can see it, preferably near your writing space.

Talisman or lucky stone

Carry or wear something that symbolises your future success. This may be something that you saw during your visualisation, or an object that somehow represents your success as a writer. It could be a crystal pendant – adventurine, citrine and amethyst are particularly good for creative work.

Remember to:

- Focus on this talisman at least once a day.
- Be thankful for anything that goes well.
- Reward yourself for the effort you put in.

Part Two
Warm Up Exercises

Taking a line for a walk

The Swiss artist Paul Klee said that drawing was 'taking a line for a walk.'

A useful warm up exercise whether you are a writer, artist or musician is to begin each day by taking a sheet of paper and finding an object that has a simple shape like a vase, a pepper pot or a cup.

This exercise works well when using a roller-ball pen or biro. Focus on the object you are looking at and follow the shape on the page with your pen. Don't lift your pen from the page, just follow the shape with your eyes and keep the pen moving. Don't look at your work until you've finished.

It is a good idea to use the same object for the 21 days and see how your technique improves as you get used to this form of focusing.

Another way of using this idea is to take a large sheet of paper and doodle with a soft pencil or piece of charcoal. Look at the shapes you've created and see if you can spot an idea or object hidden amongst the lines. Go over these sections adding more detail.

You can cut this section out with scissors and glue it onto another piece of paper or trace it and use it as the raw material for a story or picture. This could be a good way of beginning the day – or you could experiment with the poetic form of haiku.

Haiku

A haiku is a type of poetic pattern originating in Japan. It can be seen as a way of experiencing the world. It is rooted in the physical world of our senses yet suggests something deeper, usually capturing a moment in time. This form of poetry uses simple, direct language and can also be viewed as a type of meditation.

The format is as follows:

Line 1	5 syllables
Line 2	7 syllables
Line 3	5 syllables

Here are a few examples of haiku:

above traffic noise
a buzzard circles blue sky
Heaven's messenger

rain falls after snow
magic whiteness disappears
black ice covers all

plane trails and pink clouds
child's chalk lines on blue paper
shapes change as night falls

Creating a haiku at the beginning of each day can also be a good warm up exercise. These can be used later in the day to create a longer piece of writing. What begins as a haiku could become a longer poem, a flash fiction story or a section of a novel.

List of nouns

Several writers we have spoken to have said they use a list similar to this as a way of generating ideas. Add your own words, choose three, set the timer for ten minutes and see where the idea takes you.

the apple	the attic	the necklace
the frog	the letter	the secret
the dancer	the forest	the bridge

the café	the river	the beach hut
the star	the scissors	the witch
the market	the book	the doll's house
the dream	the handbag	the night train
the sunset	the candle	the cellar
the kitchen	the guitar	the gloves

A to Z of writing ideas

These are also great to use as warm up exercises. Just pick a letter of the alphabet, choose one of the prompts and begin writing as quickly as you can.

A   **Advertisements**
Look through the advertisements in your local paper. Does anything strike you as interesting? For instance – could you weave a story around 'Wedding dress Size 12 – never worn'?

Animals
Do you have a favourite animal? If so, why do you like this animal so much? Could you write a short story describing a day in the life of one of them?

B   **Balloons**
Have you always dreamed of going up in a hot air balloon? Did you love balloons when you were a child? Did you ever take part in a balloon race? Could you create a story on this theme?

Boats

Do you like travelling on boats? If so or not, write why this is true for you. Can you imagine taking a journey on a boat? If so, where would you go? What would it be like? How would the destination compare to the journey?

C ### Castles

When you look at this word, do you think of a sandcastle that you once built on a beach? Or do you think of an opulent castle in the countryside on a long stretch of emerald lawn? Write about the people and events that either image may conjure for you.

Cats

Do you love or hate cats? Why? If cats could talk, what would they say? Can you imagine a story for children or adults that would have a cat as the central character?

D ### Diamonds

What feelings does a diamond evoke for you? Love? Commitment? Passion? War? The mining industry? Write a paragraph about it, and describe in detail a person or place that comes to mind.

Dolls

Did you ever have a special doll that you really believed could talk to you? Do you have a special memory of a doll's house or a special game you played? Write about this as fully as you can.

E   **Eggs**
When you read this word, do you think of chickens?
Or do you imagine a carton with a uniform row of eggs
sitting in it? What do you notice about the surface of
an egg? Its texture, colour, opacity, shape and size may
evoke some sensory detail that you can write a
paragraph about.

Elephants
What do you know about the social life of elephants?
What parallels can be made between their social
structure and that of humans? Can you imagine a story
about a family of elephants? If so, could you tell the
story from the point of view of an elephant?

F   **France**
What thoughts, feelings, images or yearning does France
evoke for you? Have you ever been there? If so, describe
your trip. What would you like to do there if you went?

Friendly
Do you know someone who is especially friendly? Can
you plot the story of this person's life? What would their
life have been like if they weren't friendly?

G   **Garden**
What sensory experience does the word 'garden' evoke
for you? If you could have been the one to write the
novel 'The Secret Garden' what would your story be like?

Garbage

If you could spend a day in a garbage disposal plant, what items of interest might you find? Would they tell a story about their owner? Why did their owner throw them away?

H   ### Hair

Consider the life of a hairdresser – forever cutting and colouring people's hair. What kind of life stories would a hairdresser hear in one day? What would he or she make of these stories?

Hurricane

Imagine a hurricane devastating an entire town. Now imagine the impact it would have on the lives of three people who did not know each other. How would lives collide as a result? What would their stories be?

I   ### Insects

Do you find insects intriguing? Or do they give you the creeps? Do you have any early childhood stories about insects? If so, who was involved? What did they do and say? How did they react?

Infant

Do you have an infant in your home? Maybe you have cared for one – or maybe not? Either way, the word will evoke some thoughts and feelings for you. Jot these down into a paragraph.

J   ### Jealousy

Do you remember a time when you felt jealous of somebody when you were a child? How did you behave? How did the situation resolve itself?

Jade

Describe the colour and texture of a piece of jade. Imagine the life of a jade stone craftsman living in ancient China. Imagine how this person's life may be connected to a person living now, holding that stone in their hands.

K ### Kettle

Did your mother ever own a whistling kettle? What colour was it? What do you remember about it? What did you eat for breakfast when you were a child?

Kermit the frog

If Kermit the frog were to enter your writing space, what would he have to say about it? Would he have any advice to give you on any of the creative projects you are currently working on?

L ### Letter

What is the most unusual letter you have ever received? Have you ever written a letter as a therapeutic exercise and never sent it? Would it help you to heal some aspect of your life by doing this now?

Laughter

Imagine possessing the gift of comedy; being able to make people laugh non stop. Where would such a gift emerge from? Pick your favourite comedian and write a paragraph, speculating on their life story.

M **Mint**

What images does the smell of mint conjure up? Does it remind you of family Sunday dinners or does it remind you of the toothpaste you used before your first date or the sweets you bought on your way home from school?

Magic

What does this word evoke for you? If you were to write a magical tale, what would it be? Where would the story be set? Who would be the main characters?

N **Night**

Are you a day or a night person? What do you like best about night-time – e.g. the moon and stars, moths and bats and the velvet-dark sky. What don't you like about it – e.g. walking home alone?

Nervous

Imagine you're at the opera, and you see a man looking very nervous as he leaves his chair and runs up the aisle to the exit. Speculate on what's happened, where he's going and what he will find when he gets there.

O **Olives**

Imagine you are walking through an olive grove. Look at the silvery leaves and the ripening olives. What is the place like? How does this differ from an English apple orchard? Add colours, sounds and smells.

Orange

Imagine you're holding an orange in your hand. Describe in detail the appearance of the skin, its scent and what it feels like in your hand.

P   **Pathway**

Think about the pathway you have taken through life.
How many times have you reached a crossroads and not
been sure which way to go? Write about one of those
times.

Ping

What objects could the sound 'ping' apply to? Write a
short story that begins with the sound 'ping' and the
chain of events that follow.

Q   **Queen**

Did you ever play dressing up games and pretend you
were a queen or a princess? Did it make a difference to
how you walked and spoke? What did you wear? Did
you have pretend food? What was it?

Quay

Imagine a day in the life of a quay. What sort of people,
animals and objects would arrive and depart from such a
place? Imagine three of them converging on a quay at the
same time. What happens next?

R   **Rings**

This could be interpreted as the rings you wear e.g.
wedding ring, engagement ring, signet ring, the number
of rings on a doorbell or phone, circus rings or bull rings.
The choice is yours.

Rogue

If a rogue were to start work in an accounting firm, what
trouble could he/she cause? Speculate on the impact this
would have on the lives of the people working in that
firm, and its clients.

S   **Silver**
Do you prefer gold or silver? What do you associate with the colour silver – for example stars, the moon or the chocolate coins in a Christmas stocking?

Single
A single slice of cheese? A single woman? A single man? A single cherry left in a bowl? Choose any interpretation of the word 'single' and create a short story around it.

T   **Tea**
Do you use loose tea or tea bags? Have you ever tried to tell fortunes using the tea leaves left in the bottom of the cups? What happened? What if the 'fortune' you made up for somebody came true and in doing so created a new set of problems for the person?

Tiger
When William Blake wrote 'tyger, tyger, burning bright in the forest of the night, what immortal hand or eye could frame thy fearful symmetry' what did he mean? If you had to write a poem about a tiger, how would you write it?

U   **Umbrella**
Write a story featuring an umbrella. What colour is it and who does it belong to? Does it have magical properties?

Ulterior
Consider whether any of the characters in your stories have ulterior motives for their actions. If you dig deep, you will discover them. Write them down.

V   **Violet**

Could this inspire a story about a girl called Violet – or
do you remember someone who drenched themselves in
in Devon Violets perfume? Have you ever made
crystallised violets to decorate cakes?

Vein

Consider the veins in your body. Consider the veins in
a leaf. Consider veins of traffic in a large city. Consider
writing a poem about movement from one place to another.

W   **Water**

Write about water in all its disguises – waterfalls,
glaciers, mist, rain and vapour. Can you use weather in
a story to create mood and atmosphere?

Wheeze

Imagine a young man wheezing with asthma. What's
caused his asthma? How long has he had it for? What
sets it off? What must he do to control it? Does he end
up in hospital? If so, does he meet someone in there who
will change his life?

X   **X-ray**

Create the beginning of a story set in a hospital. Who is
being x-rayed and what is their problem?

Xylophone

Imagine the making of a xylophone. Where did the wood
come from? Who made it? How much money did they
get paid for it? What did they do with the money?

Garbage

If you could spend a day in a garbage disposal plant, what items of interest might you find? Would they tell a story about their owner? Why did their owner throw them away?

H ### Hair

Consider the life of a hairdresser – forever cutting and colouring people's hair. What kind of life stories would a hairdresser hear in one day? What would he or she make of these stories?

Hurricane

Imagine a hurricane devastating an entire town. Now imagine the impact it would have on the lives of three people who did not know each other. How would lives collide as a result? What would their stories be?

I ### Insects

Do you find insects intriguing? Or do they give you the creeps? Do you have any early childhood stories about insects? If so, who was involved? What did they do and say? How did they react?

Infant

Do you have an infant in your home? Maybe you have cared for one – or maybe not? Either way, the word will evoke some thoughts and feelings for you. Jot these down into a paragraph.

J ### Jealousy

Do you remember a time when you felt jealous of somebody when you were a child? How did you behave? How did the situation resolve itself?

Jade

Describe the colour and texture of a piece of jade. Imagine the life of a jade stone craftsman living in ancient China. Imagine how this person's life may be connected to a person living now, holding that stone in their hands.

K ### Kettle

Did your mother ever own a whistling kettle? What colour was it? What do you remember about it? What did you eat for breakfast when you were a child?

Kermit the frog

If Kermit the frog were to enter your writing space, what would he have to say about it? Would he have any advice to give you on any of the creative projects you are currently working on?

L ### Letter

What is the most unusual letter you have ever received? Have you ever written a letter as a therapeutic exercise and never sent it? Would it help you to heal some aspect of your life by doing this now?

Laughter

Imagine possessing the gift of comedy; being able to make people laugh non stop. Where would such a gift emerge from? Pick your favourite comedian and write a paragraph, speculating on their life story.

Y   Yes

Imagine you are on a bus and the person next to you turns to you and says: 'Just for today, say: 'Yes'!' What would you do?

Yak

The central character in one of your stories has a secret yearning to trek through Tibet with nothing but a yak for company. How does his/her fantasy about this journey play out on his/her mind? Does he or she have the courage to actually do it?

Z   Zucchini

Imagine growing these in your vegetable patch. What happens when you have a glut one year? What do you do with them?

Zambia

One of the characters in your novel falls in love with someone from Zambia. What is that person's back story? How will it impact on the story you are writing?

Writing games

Old photographs

Look for old photographs or postcards in charity shops. Can you develop a story from some of these? Several writers have created entire novels from photographs they have found in second hand sales and junk shops. Swap old family photos with a friend. See how many ideas you can generate.

'Let's pretend' and 'What if'

Look at how children play. If you're stuck for the ending of a story, list ten possible endings – no matter how far-fetched these might be. If you get the chance, get down on all-fours and play with a doll's house or toy farm. What would it be like if you were small enough to get inside?

Round the world

This is a variation on a game Sue used to play with her brother when they were children and couldn't get to sleep. To do it, you go through the alphabet from A – Z as follows:

'My name is Annabel, I live in America and I sell aubergines'.
'My name is Brendan, I live in Bolivia and I sell boxes.'
'My name is Claire, I live in China and I sell cakes.'
'My name is Daniel, I live in Denmark and I sell dogs.'

Go on through the alphabet, jotting down brief details, until you've got a list of 26 people. Pick two or three and see if you can make up a story about them. Where do they meet? Do they argue about something or do they fall in love?

Book or song titles

This is a great idea to try in a Library. Choose a shelf of books and pick three titles – for instance:

'The Magic Apple Tree'
'The Wild Girl'
'Autumn of Strangers'

See if you can create a story from this raw material. Alternatively, pick a CD and choose three song titles from the list of tracks.

Consequences

This works best with a group of five or six people. Everyone starts with a sheet of paper and follows the steps outlined below, with the intention of creating a consequence.

Here's what you do:

Write down a girl's name and job
fold over and pass to next person round the table
Write down a man's name and job
fold over, pass on
Write where they met
fold over, pass on
Write when they met (time of day and year)
fold over, pass on
What did he say to her?
fold over, pass on
What did she say to him?
fold over, pass on
What happened next?
pass on, open up and read.

See if you can create a story using this raw material.

Part Three
Tools to Keep You Focused

Daily prompts

Day board/inspirations board

Buy a cork board or make a padded board from a piece of hardboard covered with wadding and then fabric. The idea is that you pin something onto it everyday that inspires you. Change the board regularly so that items don't just become part of the furniture.

Items could include:

- a postcard
- a scrap of fabric in an inspiring colour
- a quote or affirmation
- a photograph
- a newspaper or magazine article
- a leaf or feather

One minute meditation

This can act as a real refresher on days when things aren't going so well or if you have a lot to do. Turn away from your computer. Close your eyes. Breathe in to a slow count of four, hold for four and breathe out to a count of four. Repeat five more times. Rub your palms together until they are warm. Place them over your closed eyes for a slow count of four. Have a good stretch and a yawn and you should feel ready to go on with your day.

Free-writing

When working on the exercises in this book, allow your ideas to flow freely. Concentrate on filling sheets of paper, not on getting things 'right.' Don't stop to think – just put down the first idea that comes into your head even if you think the words are taking you in the 'wrong' direction.

Just for now, don't worry about spelling, grammar or punctuation. That can all be tidied up later. Keep your pen moving! Don't stop. If you can't think what comes next, just write a shopping list, the words of a song or your last sentence until a fresh idea comes along.

The 'to do' list

Prepare this every night before you go to bed, so you won't lay awake thinking about everything you have to do the following day and blocking your creative thoughts. Put the list in a special place on your desk and use a clear quartz crystal as a paperweight.

When you begin work the next day, tick off the tasks as you complete them. Reward yourself for each one you achieve.

Keeping notebooks

Day book

This is the notebook or journal you carry around with you wherever you go. Most artists carry a sketchbook and will use it to draw any detail that interests them – an unusual window or a vase of flowers, a person's hands or a cat sleeping in the sun. They will usually make a note of colours, textures and the mood they were in at the time.

A writer's journal is similar to this but with more words than pictures. It may also include postcards, café menus, pressed flowers and diagrams, drafts of new poems and stories, descriptions of people and places and fragments of overheard conversation. Think of it as being like a compost bin for all of your creative ideas.

Ideas book

This is a separate book for storing ideas for the following:

- Ideas for projects you would like to work on in the future. (Don't worry if a particular idea seems a bit scary at the moment – write it down anyway).
- Information on people or organisations you could get in touch with e.g. competition or course organisers, publishers,

agents and other writers.

- Book or story titles.
- Character names and descriptions.

However, if you would prefer not to use an extra ideas book, you can always insert your ideas into your day book and identify them as ideas by either placing a coloured sticker next to them, or circling them with a brightly coloured felt tip pen.

Letting off steam pages

These can be written at any time of day. In her book 'The Artist's Way', Julia Cameron recommends that you do Morning Pages – three pages of long-hand every morning before the problems of the day have a chance to intrude. But mornings don't suit everybody, and sometimes if something upsetting has happened, it is better to take to the page and write about it at whatever time of day is convenient, rather than speaking out and making the situation worse.

We've found that a number of problems faced in this way have gone on to be published stories. Writing out the problem can lower blood pressure and also prevent you from saying something you may later regret.

Writing habits

Writing space

When we talk about 'space' we mean two things.

The first of these is the physical space you write in. Is it comfortable? Do you have enough lighting? Are the temperature, air flow and sound level to your liking? Do you need silence or music playing? Would you benefit from burning some essential oils or a scented candle? If so, what fragrance would be most appropriate to your mood or the story you are working on?

The second thing about 'space' is the space inside your head! Are you approaching your writing with a clear, uncluttered mind? If not, try some of the one minute meditations we've outlined in part? 3.

Do you have support from those around you? Have you given yourself permission to take this time to write or are you doing so feeling that you're being selfish? Notice the negative self talk and write anyway. Vincent van Gogh once said: 'If you hear a voice within you saying you cannot paint, then by all means paint and the voice will be silent.'

Writing regularly

Allocate some time to write every single day. Aim for fifteen minutes. If you have a busy schedule, it doesn't matter if you do this in five minute 'bites'. If necessary, lock yourself in the bathroom to do it! Don't worry about whether it's any good, just do it anyway, because it will free you up and get you into the flow of writing. If you write 300 words a day, this will add up to 109,500 words in a year! Reward yourself for the effort you put in.

Sending work off

Always keep accurate records of which pieces of writing you've sent to whom, and when. Don't keep all your eggs in one basket – send your work to as many publishers and agents as you wish. Aim to have at least ten pieces of work in circulation to begin with. Build your writing C.V. Start thinking like a writer and believe that you are one!

Celebrate every success or step forward, no matter how small.

Dealing with rejection

Creative writing is a competitive business. You can expect rejection, and lots of it, before – and after – you're published. But it doesn't matter. Look on it as part of your apprenticeship as a writer. Some writers have wallpapered their studios with the rejection letters they've received! All that matters is that you just keep writing and sending your work out.

Keeping going

Never give up. If you've read this book, this far, you obviously have a strong urge to unlock your creativity and start writing. So once you start, don't stop. Keep going.

Take a few moments each day to focus on your goals. Do one thing a day that will move you that little bit closer.

This could include:

- Create a success collage
- Find a writing buddy who will help and encourage you
- Create a profile for yourself on Twitter or Facebook
- Research possible markets for the book you are writing
- Take out a subscription to a writing magazine
- Reward yourself

Rewarding yourself

Early in your writing process, it can be helpful to decide when to treat yourself with, and with what. For instance, you may treat yourself to a chocolate cookie after writing 1,000 words.

Alternatively, if you are trying to lose weight, you may decide to buy yourself a book or some luxurious bubble bath every time you complete 5,000 words, or go for a relaxing massage.

Someone that we know buys little things that take her fancy – notebooks and pens, scented candles and hand cream. She wraps them up like presents and puts them in a drawer of her writing desk. When she feels as if she's earned a treat, she pours a glass of wine and ceremoniously unwraps one of them.

Encouraging others

When you encourage others to open up to their own creativity, and to stick with their creative goals, you remind yourself to do the same. Positive energy really helps to get things done as well as creating a nurturing atmosphere.

Mind maps

A mind map is a diagram, a visual tool for capturing ideas and associated thoughts in one picture. For visual thinkers and visual learners, the mind map is an essential tool for any project. A mind map will allow you to follow your natural tangential thought processes, and to visually describe how one idea leads to another.

Some people refer to mind maps as 'spider diagrams', because, like a spider, these maps have a central line (which is your core idea) and a number of arterial lines running off it, capturing the other ideas associated with your central idea.

We've listed a few book references on mind maps, at the end of this book, but before you spend any money on them, please have a look at the explanation and images of mind maps here: http://en.wikipedia.org/wiki/Mind_map.

Blogs

As an emerging writer, you may find that setting up your own blog is a brilliant way to get started, especially when other people find your writing interesting enough to subscribe to and comment on. It also helps to keep you focused on writing a little bit every day. We've listed some information on blogs at the end of this book, but in the meantime, do have a read of this explanation here: http://en.wikipedia.org/wiki/Blog

Part Four
21 Days of Creative Boosts

Some things to keep in mind...

As a creative person, you need ideas to keep you stimulated, or your creative well will run dry. If you have a project to finish, this can feel like trying to run a car with no petrol. We've created 21 experiences, to be used over 21 days, to help you get into the habit of writing about everyday happenings, using all of your senses, to re-ignite your creative spark.

You don't need to do these in the order outlined. In fact it would be best that you select one of these experiences to support the kind of day you're having. For instance, if you're heading out for a walk in the forest, then skip ahead to 'day 6 – a walk in the forest' and do those writing exercises. The main thing is that you take on one of these experiences every single day, and that you write about it.

We've designed 21 exercises, and four of these relate to the four seasons. So to complete one exercise every day, over a 21 period, you may need to repeat a few of them. This in itself will be an interesting exercise, as you may get completely different results the second time around! If for some reason you miss a day, don't worry about it; just get stuck into it again the next day. These exercises are designed to enliven you, not to make you feel bad in any way. We are so aware that many people's creativity is stifled by feelings of guilt, self recrimination and generally feeling 'not good enough', so it's our sincere hope that you will let go of all negative self talk and embrace the opportunity to enjoy these exercises.

You'll get the best value from these exercises if you remember to bring a notebook and pen with you to record your observations, and any extra insights and ideas that may emerge in the process. Remember to use of all the senses in your writing, as this will help to develop your skills as a writer. Failing to engage the senses is listed as one of the key reasons for manuscripts being rejected by publishers.

We have one last piece of advice for you before you dive in – stay focused on your success collage and your personal mantra.

Don't show your work to anyone until you feel happy to do so. If you do attract any unhelpful or unsupportive comments, then follow this up with a positive affirmation as quickly as you can. Nurture your creative self and value the work you are doing. You won't regret it.

OK, time to dive right in now, and enjoy ....

Day 1 – in your writing space and at the shops

What you will need:

- Time alone in your writing space
- A music playing device (CD player, iPod, MP3 player, internet etc)
- Something you like touching (e.g. a piece of velvet, satin or wool)
- Time to walk into the High Street or any shopping area

See

Take a few moments to stand in front of the collage for success that you have made. Look at the entire picture – all around the edges, the composition as a whole, each individual image and then the whole again. What story is it telling you? Write a paragraph to summarise it, as though writing the blurb on the back of a book.

Hear

Listen to a song that was your favourite at an earlier stage of your life. Keep your eyes closed while listening. What do you remember about that time? What were you wearing?

Touch

List three things you like the feel of and three things that you don't like touching. Choose one from each list and write about them as fully as you can.

Smell

Browse in a perfume shop. Is there a particular scent that conjures up a memory – for example the lavender perfume your grandmother used to wear? Write about an incident connected with this.

Taste

Buy a variety of chocolate you don't usually eat. Find somewhere to sit or lie in a relaxed position. Close your eyes. Eat the chocolate slowly, and then record any ideas or observations.

Day 2 – at an art gallery

You will need:

- Your journal and a pen
- A couple of hours to spend at an art gallery
- Some money to buy lunch at the café

See

Visit a gallery on your own and spend at least ten minutes focusing on one of the paintings. Imagine yourself stepping into the picture. What are the predominant colours? Do these colours have a special association for you? Make any notes that may be useful to you later on. Buy a postcard of the painting or take a photo.

Hear

Take a seat in the gallery and close your eyes. Listen to the sounds around you. It may be the slow shuffling of people's feet and the gentle murmur of people making comments on the paintings. Or you may hear other things. Describe these sounds, writing your descriptions into your journal. Do they remind you of anything? If so, write a paragraph about that too.

Touch

You may have a gallery pamphlet or ticket in your hand right now. Slide your fingers over it, both sides and the edge, and notice the different sensations. Describe those differences in your journal. For instance you may come up with 'rough' and smooth' and these differences may remind you of something else. Write about that too.

Smell

Notice the smells around you. They may be floor polish, perfume, wood, paint or any other substance. There will of course be many smells around you. Try to distinguish one from the other and write a few lines on each one. Then write a few lines on the experience of all of them together.

Taste

Go to the café and order a hot drink and some food. If you order something that is similar to what you would often eat and drink, then allow your mind to daydream about other cafés you have visited. Could one of these be a setting for a story?

Day 3 – anywhere comfortable

You will need:

- Your journal and pen
- A comfortable place to sit where you won't be disturbed
- Time to walk through your High Street or any shopping area

See

Sitting comfortably, let your eyes gaze out the window, all the way to the furthest point on the horizon. What do you see? Is there a sharp, clear horizon line, or is it fuzzy and cloudy? Who and what might be there at that particular point on the horizon? What are they doing? Write a paragraph about them.

Hear

Sit quietly and close your eyes. Listen to the sounds around you. It may be rain falling on your roof or tapping on your window, or it may be traffic in the distance, or the sound of the TV. Whatever it is, listen to it fully. What memories or feelings does this evoke for you? Write a paragraph about it.

Touch

Take a moment to notice how your skin feels. Is there a cool or warm breeze blowing over it? Or maybe the air around your skin is still. Notice how it feels right now, in this moment, and describe it in writing. Be poetic if you can.

Smell

Walk through your shopping centre or High Street and notice the smells emanating from the shops. What are they? If it smells like food cooking, try to identify what sort of food it is. Can you remember a time that you've smelled this before? If so, where were you, what were you doing and who were you with?

Taste

Try a new type of coffee or tea. Bring it to a comfortable chair, sit and sip. As the warm liquid rolls across your tongue and down your throat, close your eyes and savour the taste. Can you describe it? Does it evoke a memory of a place or person?

Day 4 – in your writing space

You will need:

- Your journal and pen
- A music playing device and some music you like
- Sandalwood (incense stick, cone or oil and burner)
- A cup of jasmine tea

See

You may be ready to start an art journal, or to start incorporating art into your existing journal. We often find this second option to be the best, as it helps us to integrate our creative inspirations.

Either way, start to collect images that seem to exemplify the characters, things or places which you wish to write about. Arrange those images in a composition that feels meaningful for you and stick them to the page. Paint, draw and write around or across the images in any way that feels right for you.

For some extra guidance and inspiration, go to 'Google', select 'You Tube' and type 'art journal' into the search bar. You will find an ocean of inspiration in there!

Hear

Listen to music as you're working on your art journal. It may be an old favourite or something new. Whatever you feel like playing is fine. As you work through your art journal, notice how different sounds, rhythms and speeds of music will affect the artwork you are creating. Describe these differences and the influence they're having on you.

Touch

Run your fingers over the surface of your art journal. Are there any irregularities caused by the glue or other materials you may have used? Is the surface undulating, like a hilly landscape or the waves of an ocean? If so, create a haiku about this.

Smell

Take time out now to meditate with the scent of sandalwood. You can use an incense stick, an incense cone or place a few drops of sandalwood in your oil burner.

You may wish to meditate in silence, or to follow a guided meditation on CD, MP3 or 'You Tube'. Whatever you choose, remember to put on something warm, and then sit or lie comfortably. Focus on your breathing and progressively relax every muscle in your body.

Notice the scent of the sandalwood. Don't think about it, or analyse it much, just notice it. Feel the scent moving through your mind and your body deeply relaxing you.

When you have finished your meditation, pick up your journal and describe the effect this scent had on you. Was it calming or stimulating? Did it evoke other experiences or wishes? Write about these.

Taste

Sip from a cup of jasmine tea that you have previously made. It may be green tea with jasmine or plain jasmine tea. Even if you're not a tea drinker, just try this, because the unfamiliar taste will stimulate the senses. Can you describe the flavour of the jasmine? Does it complement the scent of the sandalwood? Is this combination of scent and taste evoking a thought, feeling, memory or desire within you? If so, what is it? Write about it.

Day 5 – lunch in a café

You will need:

- Your journal and pen
- Money to buy your lunch

See

Order whatever takes your fancy. When the food and drink is brought to your table, what does it look like? Has it been arranged lovingly or artfully? Or has it been slopped onto the plate in any old fashion? What about the drink? If it's a hot drink, what kind of cup is it in? Is the shape of the cup arty, smooth, square or plain and unremarkable? If it's a cold drink, is it in a glass that is plain or one that is interesting in some way?

Pay attention to any thoughts and feelings that this visual

stimulation may evoke in you. Do the shapes, colours and textures of the food and drink and the implements inspire you in any way? Do they remind you of a past experience? Do they evoke in you a desire to paint or write about them?

Smell

How does your food and drink smell? Is it exactly as you'd expect it to smell? Or is there a certain something unexpected? Can you distinguish the various smells from each other and describe each one in turn? Do any of these smells remind you of anything? Write about it.

Taste

Does your food and drink taste as you'd expect it to? Or is there a surprise? Or is it disappointing? What about the texture of the food? Is it as good or bad as the taste of the food? Can you distinguish one from the other? Do they complement each other? Is there anything about the taste or texture of your food or drink that reminds you of a past experience or a secret wish? Write about it.

Hear

Take a moment to put down your pen and listen to the sounds around you. Can you hear the movement of people who work in the café? Is there radio playing? Is there any form of music playing? Are any of the other patrons chatting? Can you make out what they're talking about? Can you hear traffic? There may be a cacophony of sounds around you, or it may be fairly quiet. Pick up your pen and describe the sounds around you.

Touch

Right now, your hands may be touching the surface of a polished wooden table, or a glass table, or a tablecloth. Gently slide your fingers over the surface and notice how it feels. Does the sensation remind you of anything? Does it trigger any thoughts, feelings or wishes? Write about it in your journal.

Day 6 – a walk through the forest

You will need:

- Your journal and pen (or a small sound recording device)
- Clothing suitable for the weather and the terrain
- Boiled sweet (eg menthol, honey & lemon or eucalyptus)
- Optional – camera, art materials

See

Notice the variety of shapes and colour as you walk through the forest. Notice the changes in density. In parts it will be thick and lush and in other parts it will thin out. Is there mist ahead of you, or is the view clear? Notice the mood that different parts of the forest will evoke. Some parts may appear mysterious or even a bit scary, whilst other parts will appear cheerful and inviting. Does it inspire you to write a story? If so, would that story be a fairytale? Or would it be about the life of deer? Or would you be interested in writing about a reclusive person living in a tiny cottage in the deepest part of the forest?

Hear

As you walk through the forest, notice any sounds. You may hear your own feet squelching through mud, or over cracking fallen branches. You may hear the scurrying sound of small animals darting into the undergrowth as you walk by. You may hear birds in the trees. You may hear squirrels chattering at each other. Or you may hear the distant hum of traffic. Whatever the sounds are, take a moment to stop and write about them in your journal, or if you prefer, speak into a sound recording device.

Touch

As you have stopped for a moment, reach out and touch something (as long as it's not a stinging nettle!) This may be the bark of a tree or some leaves. It may be moss or a mushroom. Touch something, anything that you feel comfortable touching. Is the texture smooth or rough? Is it fine and delicate or does it feel tough? Is it both fine and tough? It is rigid or flexible?

Smell

What can you smell right now? Is there a smell of damp vegetation? Are any of the flowers or leaves releasing a smell? If so, how would you describe it? What does it evoke for you?

Taste

Put a boiled sweet into your mouth and suck it slowly as you continue walking. Let the flavour roll across your tongue. Is the flavour strong enough to reach your sense of smell? Or is it localised? What does the flavour remind you of? How would you relate this flavour to the place you are walking through now right now? Does it release any memories?

Day 7 – at the cinema

You will need:

- Your journal and pen
- A small torch, or some other light source (eg your mobile phone)
- Some of your favourite movie-eating food and drink (sweets, popcorn and coke)
- A cinema ticket and a seat far away from everyone else

See

Notice the visual aspect of the film. Is there a consistent palette of colour throughout? Are there a number of scenes filmed in nature, or is it mostly indoors? Are the actors wearing a limited range of clothes and colours? Do 'colourful characters' wear colourful clothes? What does this do to inform your thinking on any story you may be working on?

Hear
Have you noticed the music in the film? Has it enhanced the mood of the narrative in any way? If yes, how has it done this? Can you write words to describe this music?

Touch
As you are sitting in semi darkness, your sense of touch will be heightened. Run your fingers over the fabric of your seat. Is it rough and flat? Or is it soft? Can you guess what kind of fabric it is without looking at it? Is it velvet or heavy cotton or some other fibre? Is there a feeling or memory that this sensation evokes?

Smell
Notice the smells around you. Is it the smell of freshly cleaned carpet? Or is it the smell of someone's perfume or aftershave? Can you link the sense of smell to the touch of the fabric? For instance, are you sensing velvet and a deep woody perfume at the same time? If so, can you imagine one of your characters embodying these qualities?

Taste
Notice the taste and texture of the food you put in your mouth. If it's a Malteser for instance, notice the way the chocolate coating melts on your tongue before disappearing down your throat. Can you taste more than sugar? Can you also taste the cocoa beans? The remaining ball of crunchy honeycomb stuff might also have a certain texture on your tongue that is interesting. Does this taste and texture remind you of a childhood memory? Or perhaps it

reminds you of your first date with someone special. Whatever it is, write about it.

Day 8 – in your workplace

You may work in an office, or a shop or a factory or an airport. It doesn't much matter where you work, because everything around you can be used as inspiration for your creative unfolding. And no matter where you work, you are entitled to take breaks to do something enjoyable for yourself. So here's a little exercise we've put together for you to do on your lunch break.

You will need:

- A short time out from the usual routine of your job, whatever it may be
- A tissue or handkerchief with a dab of essential oil on it (preferably something stimulating like basil or orange)
- Your journal and a pen

See

Sit quietly, away from your colleagues and casually look around you. Take it all in. Notice the actions of the people nearby. Describe their movements and their facial expressions. Do they look stressed, angry, irritated or bored? Write it all down, preferably without naming people.

Hear

What can you hear? Is it traffic, or machinery or people chatting? Or is it laughter, photocopiers, telephones, computer applications running or music playing? Can you separate one noise from another and write about each one in turn? Can you also write a paragraph about the combined sound? What would an alien visitor from another planet make of it?

Touch

You may be wearing a uniform, or a suit or jeans and a jumper. Whatever you are wearing, you have probably desensitised to the feel of it because you wear it so often. Now is a chance to re-sensitise to what you are wearing. How does it feel against your skin? What does the weight of the fabric feel like on and around your body? Do you feel nurtured by these clothes? Do the colours express you? Are your shoes comfortable?

Smell

Remove the scented tissue or handkerchief from your pocket and hold it to your nose. Inhale deeply. Can you describe this smell? Does this new smell alter your perception of this familiar environment? Does this bringing together of old and new evoke any interesting memories or desires? If so, write about them.

Taste

Eat your lunch now. It may be something you have often, or you may have decided to try something new. Notice the flavours and textures as the food and liquid moves around in your mouth. Is your sense of taste in any way altered from breathing in the oils? If so, can you describe the sensation?

Day 9 – on a train

You will need:

- Your journal and a pen
- A comfortable seat on the train (we'll keep our fingers crossed you get one!)

See

Notice the other people on the train. You may or may not be able to stare, depending on how close other people are standing and sitting, but try to explore the expressions on the faces of the other passengers. If you are travelling through the countryside you may prefer to stare out of the window at the passing scenery. Or if you're on the underground, you may only catch glimpses of the advertisements on the walls at each stop. Can these fleeting images be stitched together into a lively paragraph expressing your experience on the train?

Hear

Notice the sounds around you too. You may hear the sound of the train moving along the tracks. You may also hear the sound of other people talking, or the sound of someone's music which they are playing so loudly that even with their tiny earphones stuffed into their ears, you can still hear it. Is there a way of synthesising these sounds into one single experience that you can describe in writing?

Touch

You may have your hand on some kind of railing to steady your balance. It may be cold metal or it may be warm and painted. It may feel unclean, or it may not. The fabric of the seat you're sitting on may also have a certain tactile quality which you can describe. Is there any airflow in this train or is the atmosphere hot and stuffy? Whatever the case, describe it, and how it impacts on the train riding experience.

Smell

You may be surrounded by the smell of other people on the train. Some may smell of a pleasant perfume or aftershave. Others may smell neutral whilst others still may smell very unpleasant to you. What do these smells do to your overall experience?

Taste

You may wish to put a boiled sweet or some chewing gum into your mouth right now; either as a distraction, or just because you like it. Does this flavour trigger work with your other senses to generate any particular memory or desire? If so, jot it down now.

Day 10 – standing in a queue

Unless you live alone on a remote island, the chances are you spend time standing in queues. It may be a queue in the post office, or the bank, or the newsagent, or the supermarket or at the bar. One way or another, you will at times encounter queues. Many people find them exasperating and frustrating, but they don't have to be, at least, not if you use them as research for your creative writing.

You will need:

- Your journal and a pen.
- Comfortable shoes!

See

Notice the people ahead of you. Do they look bored or quite happy standing there? Do their facial expressions change as they get closer to the head of the queue? What about the people on the receiving end of the queue? Do they seem stressed, or quite happy to take one customer at a time without any problem? What about the environment in which you are standing? Is the ceiling high or low? Is the building old or new? Are the colours to your liking, or are they completely dreary? Whatever the case, describe the scene in detail.

Hear

Can you hear the conversation of other people standing in the queue? Can you hear the conversations between customer and person working at the other end of the queue? If so, are those conversations light and polite? Or is there something more interesting being discussed? Can you describe the tones and qualities in the voices? Are they silken, or bristling? What other sounds are around you?

Touch

Are you holding something in your hand? It may be money or letters. What is the texture like? Can you see or hear something that combines in an interesting way with your sense of touch? For instance, do the gravelly tones of the old man in front of you correspond with your experience of the rough textured envelope in your hands? Does he remind you of a character you would like to write about? Could he be the grandfather or the main character in a story you are writing?

Smell

Is there a certain smell in this place? It may smell of paint, or new carpet or beer. Whatever it is, notice the smells and how they impact on your experience of the place. Would the main character in your book love or hate any of these smells?

Taste

It can be helpful to chew gum when you're standing in a queue as it keeps you awake. Or you may be eating or drinking something. If so, does it distract you from the experience? Is this something the teenager in the skimpy outfit at the front of the queue would eat? Can you imagine her preferences, if you were writing about her?

Day 11 – if you're having a blue day

In part three we talked about the importance of keeping notebooks and journals. We mentioned that you may even wish to have several, including one for 'letting off steam'. But sometimes letting off steam just isn't enough, and sometimes you simply don't have any steam to let off. You may instead just feel a bit flat. You may, or may not, know the reason for this sadness.

Writing from this emotional space can actually be quite powerful, so anytime you're having a blue day try this exercise.

You will need:

- Your journal and a pen
- A comfortable and private place
- A few drops of orange essential oil in a burner
- A smooth river stone, preferably the size of your palm
- A cup of lemon and ginger tea
- Tissues

See

Close your eyes and relax, focusing on your breathing. Allow your breathing to slow down to a series of slow deep inhalations and exhalations. With every exhalation, feel the tension leaving your body. Bring your awareness deep inside your body.

Imagine a very tiny version of yourself moving through your body, seeking the part of you that feels sad. You may find the sadness around your heart, or your throat or lungs. You may find the sadness in your stomach or intestines, your pelvic region or even in your joints. It may be anywhere, so take your time to find it.

Each time you find a sad spot, bless it and cast a warm orange light around it. Open your eyes down and write a paragraph on the voyage within, from the point of view of the tiny being who has just travelled around inside you. What did the tiny being see, feel and do in there? Write about this in as much detail as you can.

Touch

Open your eyes again and pick up the smooth river stone you've brought into this space. Place the smoothest surface in the palm of your hand. Notice how it feels against your skin, and whether it evokes any imagery for you. Now wrap your other hand over the top of the stone, enclosing it comfortably between your hands.

Close your eyes now, and visualise any residual sad feelings travelling out of your body, down your arms, through the palms of your hands into this stone. Visualise the sadness as waves of deep blue energy leaving your body and seeping into the stone. Remain in this space for as long as you need to; as long as it takes for all the sadness to leave your body.

Then open your eyes and write about how your body feels.

Smell

Notice the smell of the orange essential oil burning in the room. Let the scent and the colour fill you. What does the colour orange remind you of? Does it evoke any new ideas or desires? Write a paragraph about it.

Taste

Take a sip from the cup of lemon and ginger tea you made earlier. It should now be cool enough for you to allow it to move around your tongue for a moment before you swallow it. Can you isolate the flavour of each – lemon and ginger – and notice how they interact with each other? Does one dominate the other? Or are they well balanced? What effect does each have on you? Do you know any stories about the medicinal benefits of each? If so, where did you hear them from? Can you recall a time, place or person who shared this knowledge with you? What were you wearing that day? Where were you?

Hear

Keeping your eyes closed, notice the sounds around you. Now matter how high or low the volume of sound is, no matter how many or how few sounds surround you, just notice them. Does each sound have a colour associated with it? Does each sound have a certain rhythm associated with it? Does each sound evoke a sense of movement or stillness? Write a short poem about this.

Day 12 – observing Autumn

Whether you love or hate autumn, you'll notice it stirs up a number of feelings, usually feelings influenced by your past. Autumn is a reflective time of year; a time to harvest whatever you've sown throughout the year, and to prepare for the incubation of winter. For all of these reasons, it's an excellent time to write!

You will need:

- Your journal and a pen
- A comfortable and private place
- A few drops of orange and sage essential oils in a burner
- A collection of autumn-like objects including leaves and other things from nature, wet clay, colourful pictures from a magazine, and a ball of wool.
- A warm drink of your choice

See

Sit comfortably on the floor, or at a table, with all of your autumn props scattered before you. Then, without thinking about it too much, arrange them into a composition which you find pleasing. This may be a three dimensional structure, or it may be a layout for a picture.

Once you've arranged them to your liking, stand up and slowly walk around your creation, observing it from a number of angles. What does it tell you about autumn? Photograph it and then write a paragraph about it, as though you are an artist selling this piece of work in a gallery.

Hear

Now dismantle your creation and start to rearrange it. As you do so, notice the sound of the objects. If you have leaves or other organic forms, they may snap and crackle as you move them. If you have paper or magazines, they may make a slapping sound as you move them. If you have clay it may make a squelching sound, and so on. Notice the sounds of movement and describe them in a short, poetic paragraph.

Touch

Once you have rearranged the objects to create a different composition, walk around your composition a few times without looking at it. Stop, close your eyes and then reach your hands over to your composition. Feel the different textures in it. There will be rough and smooth sensations. There will be wet and dry textures. There will be warm and cool textures. Notice the contrasting sensations and then write a paragraph about them.

Smell

Exit the space for a moment and then return again, closing the door behind you. Do you notice the scent of the orange and sage burning? Can you identify each scent in turn? Can you describe the combined scent? Does it evoke a memory? Does it evoke a new idea or desire? Write about it.

Taste

Sip your warm drink now, and notice whether it tastes any different to usual. Is your sense of taste heightened by the scent of the orange and sage? If so, what does it evoke? Write about it.

Day 13 – observing Winter

If you're in the depths of winter, and feeling it, you may enjoy this exercise.

You will need:

- Your journal and a pen
- Warm clothes for wearing outdoors
- A few drops of frankincense or sandalwood essential oil in a burner

- A comfortable and private place
- A warm drink of your choice

See

Go for a brisk walk outside. If it's icy or snowy, please be careful! As you walk, keep your head up and look all round you. Depending on where you are, you may see nothing but an open field covered in snow, or a crowd of people walking through the city centre. Wherever you are – is there a sense of joy or anticipation? Or is there a sense of retreat and slumber? What colours to you see? Scuttle back indoors and write about it.

Hear

What sounds did you observe on your outing? Traffic? People laughing? Or was it dead silent? Are these sounds indicative of winter? Or do they juxtapose your feelings about winter? Why? What are the words you would use to describe winter?

Taste

Sip a warm drink of your choice. Does this drink taste different in winter than it does in summer? Does your feeling about winter impact your sense of taste? What time of year was it when you first tasted this drink? Can you remember who you were with and what you were doing?

Touch

Notice the sensation of the skin on your hand where it is touching the warm cup. Is your hand warmer than the rest of your body? Or is the temperature evenly distributed now? Can you remember a time when you were really cold, so cold you were collapsed in the middle? Where were you? What were you doing? Were you waiting for someone?

Smell

Close your eyes now and breathe deeply. Exhale slowly and fully. Notice the scent of the essential oils filling your mind. Notice how this scent makes you feel calm in the centre of your being.

Stay in this place for a few moments, noticing how good it feels. Allow random thoughts to flit into your mind and leave again. Continue to breathe into the depth of your being. Slowly exhale again. Open your eyes and quickly jot down those random thoughts that came and went. What did they look like, sound like, feel like? Were they 'must do' tasks? Were there important reminders or flashes of inspiration about your creative desires? Write about it, as though you are relaying an important message to someone else.

Day 14 – observing Spring

When spring has sprung, you know it. There's sunshine, there's a fresh scent in the air, the trees are bursting with new growth and colourful blossoms, and there is good cheer all around you.

You will need:

- Your journal and a pen
- Suitable clothes for wearing outdoors
- A few drops of jasmine essential oil in a burner
- A comfortable and private place
- A glass of apple juice
- Optional – a camera

See

Go for a walk in a public garden or park. Notice the sense of joy and anticipation around you. Notice the abundance of colour in the foliage and in other people's clothes. Imagine yourself inside a computer-generated movie. Describe what this place would look like if you were flying through the air.

Hear

Close your eyes and listen to the sound of your wings; their rapid movement causing a high pitched hum. Listen to the sound, and then listen through the sound to hear the sounds of people and other life around you. Is it a wild cacophony of sounds? Or are there a few, easy to distinguish sounds? Describe them.

Touch

Run your hand down the bark of a tree, or over some grass or along a park bench or along a brick wall. Make use of whatever you have access to. If possible, take photographs of the different surfaces you touch (to print later and make a collage from).

Do any of these surfaces evoke in you a memory of the first time you ever touched this substance? If so, where were you, who were with and how did this texture feel? Does it feel the same now? Write a short poem about the sensation.

Smell

Return home to your writing space and light the oil burner with a few drops of jasmine in it. Sit quietly adding to your notes and/or looking through any photographs you took. Is there a collective experience of spring starting to come together? Are you able to 'package' it into a short poem? Or are you sensing the beginning of a novel?

Either way, try to identify the key elements of this emerging piece of writing by jotting down people, places and a sketchy narrative. By the time you've done this, you'll start to notice the scent of jasmine filling the room. Close your eyes and breathe it in. Feel the sense of anticipation it evokes. Feel excited about your new creative writing project.

Taste

Sip the apple juice. Close your eyes and let it flow all around your tongue. Quickly jot down three adjectives that come to mind.

Don't think about it for too long. Just write down the first three words you think of.

Now sit back and observe all of the elements of your spring experience – flight, movement, colours, sounds, textures, scents and tastes – and keep building on it. A story will start to take shape very soon.

Day 15 – observing Summer

At the high point of summer, try this exercise.

You will need:

- Your journal and a pen
- Suitable clothes for wearing to the beach
- A few drops of rose essential oil in a burner
- A comfortable and private place
- A glass of elderflower cordial
- Optional – a camera

See

Even if you live far from the beach, make the effort to go at least once this summer, as the experience can be very stimulating for creative writers. Walk along the beach, being sure to let the water lap over your bare feet. Look at everything around you – the sand, the shells and pebbles, other people and their dogs.

Then sit down for a moment and stare at the horizon line. Notice how it feels to look that far into the distance. Does it inspire a story about a journey – or something else? Whatever it evokes, write it down now.

Hear

Listen to all of the sounds around you, including the sound of the ocean, seagulls, voices, dogs barking, maybe even traffic in the distance, or perhaps music. Jot down all of the sounds and describe the interplay between them.

Do these sounds remind you of a childhood holiday on the beach? Write down everything you remember about a particular day.

Touch
Grab a handful of sand. Hold it tight and loosen your grip ever so slightly until every grain of sand has fallen from your hand. Repeat the procedure three times, noticing how it feels on your skin and in your muscles. Create a short poem about the sensation.

Smell
Back home in your writing space, place a few drops of rose essential oil into an oil burner and light the candle. As the burner is warming up, assemble your notes and photographs and sketch out a story about a character that lives on the beach.

By now the scent of the rose oil should be filling the room. Close your eyes and breathe in the scent deeply. Is the scent warm and deep? Or are there some other words that you would use to describe it? Can you weave these into the story you are writing about summer?

Taste
Sip the elderflower cordial with your eyes closed. Allow the liquid to flow around your tongue before you swallow it. Open your eyes and jot down three words to describe the feeling.

Add these descriptions to the collection of sensory images you have for your new story – or use them to enhance something you're already working on. They may form part of the back story for a particular character.

Day 16 – upon waking
Like many creative people, you may have a rich and vivid inner world when you sleep. No doubt, you dream prolifically, and

although you may not always recall your dreams, you will find that you soon start to recall them when you get into the habit of writing the instant you wake up.

Julia Cameron's landmark book 'The Artist's Way' prescribed an exercise called 'the morning pages' which asked the reader to pick up pen and paper immediately upon waking, and write three pages of longhand because it captures the stream of consciousness that is present before your fully awoken critical and judging mind kicks in. Based on this same principle, we are suggesting this structured exercise below.

Please sit up the instant you wake, pick up your pen and start writing in your journal. Don't stop to think about something clever to write. Just write, even if it's stuff like "my eyes are blurry and I can't see what I'm writing..."

You will need:

- Your journal and pen beside your bed ready for when you wake up

See

Write everything you see. It may only be your hand on the paper, but write it anyway. You may quickly recall a dream you've just had, so write about what you saw.

Hear

Write down everything you hear, no matter what it is, even if it's silence. Write about it, what it sounds like. And if you're recalling a dream you've had, write about the sounds in the dream. Were they associated with any movements or actions?

Touch

Write what your sense of touch is experiencing right now. It may be the feel of your bed sheets on your skin, it may be the temperature of the air around you or it may be something else.

Whatever it is, just write about it. If you recall a dream, write about the sense of touch in the dream, especially if it's about a person, animal or object.

Smell
What do you smell right now? Describe it in full. Does it make you hungry? Does it remind you of anything? Were there any smells in your dream?

Taste
Can you taste anything right now? Were you eating anything in your dream – for example a hotdog or a medieval banquet? If so, write down everything you can remember about this.

Day 17 – an extra long shower
You will need:

- Extra long shower time, uninterrupted
- Your journal and pen – placed right next to your towel so you can use them straight away.

See
Take an extra long shower, uninterrupted, close your eyes and enjoy the hot water steam and scents in the shower recess. Enjoy this bliss for a few minutes, and then slowly open your eyes. Notice what you see. It may only be steam, wet tiles and your toenails, but notice how everything looks. Can you imagine a poem that would succinctly describe these sights?

Hear
Notice what you can hear. It may be music playing, birds outside the window, or traffic, or just the sound of water falling. Can you find some interesting words to describe the sound? Could any of these images and ideas form the first draft of a poem?

Touch

You will have no trouble noticing how your skin feels whilst in the shower. It may feel oily or squeaky clean, and of course it will feel wet and warm. Can you come up with some poetic descriptions for the feeling?

Smell

Notice the scent inside the shower recess. You will probably be using shampoo, conditioner and skin wash. Notice the smell of each one, one at a time, and then consider how the scent makes you feel. Does it remind you of anything? Does it evoke any new ideas or desires?

Taste

Open your mouth. Let it fill with water, swish it around and spit it out. Is there any residual taste in your mouth? If so describe it.

Day 18 – at a party

You will need:

- A pen and a small notebook which you can use in the loo, or somewhere private!

See

Observe the people around you. Notice their posture, facial expressions, clothes and movements. Is there anything you see that particularly intrigues you? If so, make a mental note of it, and write in full detail when you are able to everything you noticed about that person. It may be that there is something about them that reminds you of someone else, or it may be that they are so unfamiliar to you that you're fascinated. Either way, record the details as fully as you can, as this will be useful for developing a character in one of your stories at some time in the future.

Hear

Listen to the sounds around you too. You may hear laughter. If you focus on the laughter for a moment, you may notice the wide variety of laughing sounds. Some people laugh in short, sharp bursts, whilst others are more inclined to giggle. Can you come up with some good descriptions for the different types of laughter? If so, can you link these sounds to any other qualities of the character? Make a note too, of the other sounds around you. There may be children playing, or music or the clatter of knives and forks.

Touch

Notice your sense of touch. If someone is speaking to you, they may also touch you. What does their touch feel like? Is it warm or abrasive? How do your clothes feel against your skin? Is there a cool breeze blowing or is the air around you warm? If you're at a crowded party, you may have to squeeze through a crowd to get to the loo or to move from one room to another. How does that feel? How does it impact on your other senses?

Smell

As you move past other people, or they move past you, you may notice the smell of their perfume or aftershave. Do any of these evoke a memory for you? Write about this in as much detail as you can. Notice the other smells around you too. They may be food or they may be from the garden or something else. Can you separate the smells and identify them, or is it more like a cacophony? Make a note of any feelings and emotions you experience.

Taste

If you're at a party, the chances are you will be eating or drinking something. Whatever it is, describe the taste of it in your mouth, and the taste it leaves behind after you've swallowed it. Does it make you happy? Does it remind you of anything, perhaps another party or social event? Or is it a completely unique taste? Is your sense of taste more difficult to access when you are surrounded by other people?

Day 19 – watching TV

You may not enjoy watching TV. You may turn your nose up at it, but as a writer, it's important to check in once in a while and see what's happening, because it can feed your writing. You could also think about the sort of programmes the characters in your story might watch – and imagine how and where they are sitting while they do so.

You will need:

- Your pen and your notebook

See

Pick a channel, any channel. Explore the 'vision' part of television by turning off the sound and just watching. What do you see? It may be a wonderful landscape, or a wall of graffiti, or people shooting each other.

Whatever it is, describe the vision in detail – the colours, the shapes and the movements – and then write about how it makes you feel. Does this vision evoke memories of having seen something similar before, or is this vision completely new to you? Can you imagine a dialogue or sound that you might play over this vision? If so, write it down.

Hear

Now turn on the volume. Does the sound and/or dialogue match up with what you imagined the programme was about? Does the introduction of sound give you new ideas? If you were asked to write a show for TV what would you do? Would one of your stories make a good TV script for a sitcom?

Touch

Notice how your television viewing may affect your body temperature. If you are watching something scary or stressful, your body temperature may drop a few degrees. But if you are watching something funny or beautiful, it may increase. If you were writing a story that was similar to the plot that you are watching right now, what descriptions would you provide for your reader, regarding the central character's sense of touch?

Smell

Imagine if you were there, inside that story and place that is being portrayed in television. What would you smell? How would your central character feel about the smell? How would they describe it? Would it remind them of anything?

Taste

Likewise, what would your central character taste if they were there, in that story? How would their sense of taste be affected by their physical surroundings? Write about this in as much detail as you can.

Day 20 – in church (or any place of worship)

It may not feel appropriate to be seen taking notes, so make as many mental notes as you can and have your notebook handy so you can quickly scribble it all down later.

You will need:

- A pen and notebook

See

Describe your physical surroundings. They may be ornate or simple, beautiful or frightening. Whatever they are, describe them in as much detail as you can. Then consider how these surroundings may look to other people, especially those that created them.

Look at the people who occupy this space right now. Do they look happy, peaceful, serious, or something else? Are they dressed and groomed in a way that makes you wonder how they might look outside of this environment? Let your imagination run free and when you get home write as much as you can about those people as potential characters.

Hear

Notice the sounds around you. You may hear chanting, singing, silence or someone speaking, or a variety of all of those sounds. What kind of vibration do these sounds have? Is it a calming and peaceful vibration? Does it make you feel safe? What do these sounds remind you of? If you close your eyes and listen to these sounds, what do you see in your mind's eye?

Touch

Notice the temperature and airflow around you. Is the temperature comfortable? Write about it. Is there movement around you? How does it make you feel? Does this place of worship have people touching each other? Or are people keeping their distance from each other?

Smell

What can you smell? It may be other people, or incense or flowers or something else. Can you describe each one? Can you identify the ways in which each one of these smells affect your experience of this place? Does smell enhance your ability to access God or Spirit? How might it affect others?

Taste

What can you taste? If there is a sharing of food, what is it like? Write about this in as much detail as you can.

Day 21 – in the classroom

Whether you are (or were) the kind of student who doodled and daydreamed in class, just take a moment now to consider how a classroom environment may influence your writing. Have a go at the exercise below, and record your findings. You may also wish to doodle.

By the way, there seems to be a fair bit of evidence emerging these days, to support the theory that doodling actually enhances our ability to concentrate on what we're hearing in a classroom environment.

You will need:

- A pen and notebook

See

You will be surrounded by many things – other people, the person at the front speaking, the walls, windows and objects around the room – record them all in detail.

Do any of these remind you of anything? How do they compare or contrast with your childhood classroom experiences? If you're being pulled towards a particular memory – go with it and write about it in full. You will have a short story in no time! Seriously, you will.

Hear

What are the sounds around you? You may hear someone speaking. This person may or may not be the teacher. Listen to others in the room too. There may be cross-conversations between a few people whilst the teacher is talking. This may be distracting, but try to listen to both and consider the relationship (or clash) between the two.

Listen also to the other sounds. You may hear traffic outside the windows, or birds in trees, or people talking in a hallway, or a waterfall. Whatever it is, write about it. Are there any sounds that would be loved or hated by the central character in any story you're writing?

Touch

Consider also what you are touching. You may have your hands on a desktop, or you may be fiddling with your pen, or the sleeve of your jumper. Whatever you are touching, notice it, and describe the sensation.

Would a character in your story enjoy this sensation? Notice also the temperature and movement of air around you. Does it influence your general well being? Does it enable you to concentrate on what's happening in this classroom? Or does it make you want to leave and retreat into another space?

Smell

Notice the smells around you. It may be coffee brewing, or the sandwich in your lunch box. Whatever the smells are, describe them. If someone has just entered a room, or walked past you, describe their smell. Does the smell fit with the way this person looks? For instance, their perfume may be sweet and floral, but they may be dressed all in black, and looking grumpy or menacing. Notice juxtapositions such as these and write about them.

Taste

Notice your sense of taste too. You may still be able to taste some food or liquid you ate or drank before entering this class. If so, how does that taste fit with your current experience of the space you are in? For instance, you may be in a pretty, floral room and yet the taste in your mouth is bitter. Consider a poem that would explore the contrast between the two. Write a haiku about it.

Part Five
Taking Care of the Writer

Self-care for writers

It is important that you look after yourself as well as you can. Writing is hard work physically, mentally and emotionally. Think about the following points as you go through each day.

- Make sure your chair is comfortable and supports your back.
- Move from your chair regularly and do some stretches – it will re-energise you!
- Rest your eyes by turning away from the computer screen and focusing on something in the distance every 45 minutes.
- Eat plenty of fruit and vegetables to keep you healthy.
- Drink lots of water.
- A daily walk will help your circulation and generate new ideas.
- Do one thing a day that makes you feel special – e.g. go for a massage or have a relaxing bath. Sandalwood is especially good for bringing about a relaxed but alert state of mind if used in a bath with a drop of rose oil and a drop of lavender oil.
- Read as widely as you can.
- Reward yourself for the effort you put into your work.
- If you're not sleeping well, try relaxing with a combination of camomile, sandalwood and lemon in an oil burner – or put a few drops of lavender on your pillow.

Aromatherapy for writers

Aromatherapy oils can be extremely useful for writers as a way of creating the right atmosphere in the writing space as well as being good for relaxation when the work is done. Lavender, for instance, is known to evoke a deep sense of relaxation. And it's very soothing for burns.

Oils that promote good concentration and aid creativity are

lemon, basil, bergamot, rosemary and geranium. Try a few drops of one of these in an oil burner the next time you have a difficult scene to write in a story or are seeking fresh inspiration.

If you need a peaceful atmosphere for visualisation try jasmine, carnation, frankincense or neroli. For a good night's sleep, a few drops of lavender, marjoram or sandalwood in a bath will work wonders – or put a few drops on your pillow.

You may find it helpful to select a particular fragrance for the story you are working on so that when you smell this, it will help you access that particular creative pathway more quickly.

What smells does your main character like and dislike and why? For instance – what if he or she has unhappy memories of staying with an aunt who had a passion for lavender but was unkind to the person when they were young? How does the person feel when they are older and they smell lavender. Could a smell unlock a childhood memory for somebody or help to solve a mystery?

Recipes for writers

As we all know, food nourishes the body and mind, and a healthy diet helps us to achieve our goals, no matter what they are. There are, however, some simple comforts which we can use as rewards to keep us motivated, at the desk writing, pushing through the tough bits that make us feel blocked.

Sometimes a simple trick like promising yourself you will have a treat after writing 2,000 words, or writing solidly for two hours, can be a powerful way of focusing the mind. And enjoying a simple treat after reaching each milestone can be incredibly satisfying. You may also wish to incorporate the actual making of your treat into your reward system.

If so, here are some recipes which we recommend because they are quick and easy, and can make your break time special. Buy yourself a cup and saucer or mug that makes you feel like a writer, and enjoy a hot drink with one of these biscuits.

Almond Biscuits

(makes about 20)

You will need:

2 cups flour

1¼ cups sugar

2 tsp almond essence

20 almonds – blanched

warm milk for kneading

¾ cup of butter

3 tbsp ground almonds

½ tsp baking powder

Steps:

Sieve flour and baking powder. Add ground almonds.

Mix sugar, butter and essence in a large bowl.

Add flour mixture and knead to stiff dough with the warm milk.

Keep covered in the fridge for half an hour.

Knead again and roll out into a ½ cm thick sheet.

Cut out the biscuits with a round cutter. Place on a baking tray.

Put a blanched almond on each biscuit.

Bake at 180 C for 15 – 20 minutes.

Cool for 2 – 3 minutes before removing from the baking tray.

Chewy Ginger Biscuits

(makes about 20)

You will need:

100 g butter

175 g caster sugar

1 egg

1½ tbsp golden syrup

250 g plain flour

½ tsp bicarbonate of soda

2 tsp ground ginger

6 oz crystallized ginger

Steps:

Preheat oven to Gas 4, 180C. Grease a baking tray.

Beat butter and sugar in a large bowl. Add egg and syrup.

Sieve the flour, bicarbonate of soda and ground ginger into the mixture.

Add the crystallized ginger.

Shape the dough into 20 walnut sized pieces.

Place on the baking tray, allowing room to spread.

Bake for 12 – 15 minutes.

Allow to cool before moving onto a wire rack.

Oat Cookies

(makes about 28)

You will need:

175 g self raising flour

75 g porridge oats

175 g granulated sugar

1 tsp bicarbonate of soda

175 g butter

2 tbsp golden syrup

Steps:

Preheat oven to Gas 4/180 C. Grease a baking tray.

Put the flour, oats, sugar, bicarbonate of soda and baking powder into a large mixing bowl.

Put butter and syrup into a pan and stir over a low heat until melted.

Pour onto dry ingredients and stir until combined.

Divide into approximately 28 walnut sized pieces.

Put on baking sheet and flatten slightly.

Bake for 12 – 15 minutes.

Lemon and Rosemary Cookies

(makes 16 – 20)

You will need:

1½ cups softened butter

1½ cups sugar

½ tsp fresh rosemary

1 tsp lemon zest

1 egg

1½ cups flour

¼ tsp baking soda

½ tsp salt

For the coating, you will need:

3 tbs sugar

1 tsp lemon zest

Steps:

Beat butter, sugar, lemon zest, rosemary and egg together with a wooden spoon.

Add flour, baking soda and salt.

Combine ingredients and form into a cylinder shape.

Refrigerate for 2 hours or until firm.

Preheat oven to 375 degrees.

Mix 3 tbs sugar and lemon zest in a shallow dish.

Roll dough cylinder in mixture to coat the outside before cooking.

Cut into slices and place on greased baking sheet.

Bake for approximately ten minutes or until the edges of the biscuits are light brown.

Lavender Biscuits

(makes 18 – 24)

You will need:

170 g plain flour

110 g butter

56 g caster sugar

2 tsp fresh lavender flowers

icing sugar to dust

Steps:

Preheat oven to 180C/Gas 4.

Cream butter and sugar.

Sprinkle in lavender flowers. Add the flour.

Mix to a soft dough and then wrap in cling film and chill for 30 minutes.

Roll out on a lightly floured surface and cut out 18 – 24 biscuits.

Put on baking tray and cook for 10 – 12 minutes.

Apricot Biscuits

(makes approx. 20)

You will need:

160 g butter

185 g caster sugar

2 tbsp marmalade

165 g chopped dried apricots

125 g self raising flour

5 tbsp plain flour

Steps:

Preheat oven to 180C/Gas 4.

Line baking tray with baking parchment.

In a large bowl, cream butter and sugar with a wooden spoon.

Add marmalade, flour and apricots.

Form mixture into a cylinder shape and wrap in cling film.

Chill for 15 minutes

Chop into rounds and place on baking tray.

Bake for 15 minutes.

Cool for a few minutes before removing from baking tray.

Chocolate Chip Cookies

(makes 12 – 15)

You will need:

115 g softened butter

70 g caster sugar

1 egg yolk

2 drops vanilla extract

150 g plain flour

40 g chocolate chips

Steps:

Preheat the oven to 180C/Gas 4. Grease a baking tray.

In a large bowl, cream butter, sugar, egg yolk and vanilla extract with a wooden spoon.

Add the flour gradually, stirring to make a thick dough.

Add the chocolate chips.

Shape the dough into walnut sized pieces and put on baking tray.

Press with finger tips to flatten into rounds.

Leave plenty of space between the biscuits.

Bake for 12 – 15 minutes until golden, but still a little soft in the middle

Part Six
Planning Ahead

Where to next?

Remember that you can repeat all or part of the 21 days at any time you feel you need a creative boost.

Look at the list of ambitions you created at the beginning of the twenty one days. Has anything changed or have you got ideas you would like to add to the list? Don't worry if some of these seem out of range or unattainable at the moment – just watch how quickly you move towards them.

Look at the answers you gave to the questions in Part 1. Have any of these changed?

Look at the collage you created at the beginning of this journey. Create another one if you need to reflect any changes that have occurred since you started working through this book.

Think again about where you would like to be in five years time. Take a few moments to visualise this as fully as you can. Use all the senses as you imagine yourself going through a typical day.

Vision creation and goal setting

You may find that, as you open more fully to your creativity, visions just come to you. If and when this happens, it's most likely to come in quiet and mundane moments, when you're least expecting it. The reason for this is that it takes the mind time to integrate new ideas, and the exercises that you discipline yourself to do each day, WILL generate new ideas. They will percolate and incubate inside you, and then erupt quite spontaneously, as visions.

A vision can be a vague and ill defined general sense like an 'aha' moment or a deep desire to make something happen. But sometimes a vision is a clear and crisp image of something that comes to you quite suddenly.

For Val, this occurred in a laundromat in Barcelona. She was staring at her washing bouncing around inside a machine and suddenly, for no particular reason, she 'saw' in her mind's eye an image of a large house in the countryside. She quickly dismissed it as irrelevant, but was surprised to find herself living in that very house some three months later when she re-read her notes about this vision, in her travel journal!

For author J K Rowling, the vision for Harry Potter and his friends came to her quite spontaneously when she was on a train. She knew then, that Harry's story would be told over seven books. And of course, that's exactly what happened.

Whatever your vision, if it is an authentic expression of a desire, or something that you are strongly committed to, then keep going until it becomes a reality. Create a collage, affirmation or painting that reminds you of this.

Make a five year plan

Break this down into bite-sized pieces that enable you to reach your goal one step at a time. Reward yourself for each step you achieve. Create your plan following the steps outlined below.

Year 1 (month 1)

If you are beginning your Five Year Plan in January, list ten things you would like to achieve by the end of that month.

For example:

- Buy a notebook or folder for the novel I want to write
- Tidy a space in the spare room so I can work in there
- Buy a new lamp for the desk
- Clear any unwanted clutter and take to charity shop
- Sort books that will help with my research
- Jot down brief ideas for characters and settings
- Create a collage
- Start to put a scrap book of photos and ideas together
- Plan writing time and put in diary
- Establish writing habit – like training for a race

Year 1 (month 3)

List ten things you would like to achieve by the end of March.

For example:

- Visit one of the locations where the novel is set and take photos
- Add to information about characters. Create detailed biographies
- Maintain regular writing sessions
- Create the blurb for the back of the book
- Set up a file on the computer for the novel
- Find a working title
- Create a 2,000 word outline
- Find a writing buddy or group
- Set up a reward system for the work I am doing
- Do basic research for the novel

Year 1 (month 6)

List ten things you would like to achieve by the end of June.

For example:

- Expand the basic outline to 10,000 words
- Break the outline down into 20 scenes
- Develop each scene into a full chapter
- Complete first draft by the end of June
- Look at research information and create at least one article
- Aim for ten short pieces of work in circulation e.g. letters, poems, flash fiction
- Create a writing C.V.
- Attend at least one author talk or book signing
- Enter two competitions
- Get a subscription to a writing magazine

Year 1 (month 9)

List ten things you would like to achieve by the end of September.

For example:

- Put first draft on one side – work on some short pieces
- Jot down notes or ideas for next book
- Think about possible settings and collect ideas
- Get active on Facebook and Twitter
- Form links with other writers
- Find a new interest that could inspire a story
- Attend a writing workshop
- Aim for 15 – 20 pieces of work in circulation
- Browse in bookshops and newsagents for information on publishers and writers
- Keep looking for new markets

Year 1 (month 12)

List ten things you would like to achieve by the end of December.

For example:

- Go back to your manuscript and revise
- Make a list of possible publishers
- Send out three more articles/stories per month
- Create a synopsis
- Seek a professional opinion on your work if necessary
- Review my writing tools
- Set up a Blog and update regularly
- Add to information I am gathering for novel number 2
- Polish novel number 1
- Create a letter to send to publishers

Wish list

Create a monthly wish list, breaking down each of the individual points still further. For instance, if one of your points was researching a novel, you could include a phone call you need to make or a place you could write to for further information.

Reward yourself for each item you complete.

Years 2 – 5

Begin planning for Year 2 when you reach the end of Year 1 – Month 9.

Allow the plan to be flexible. It is there to help and encourage you, not to act as a straitjacket!

Review your writing life at regular intervals – a bit like having an appraisal at work. Concentrate on doing what makes you happiest. If you feel passionate about the story you are writing, this will shine through.

Think like a writer

If you're new to writing, develop good habits from the start. If you value the work you are doing, whether you are published or not, then those around you will respect it. Don't show your work to anyone until you feel happy to do so. Don't keep talking about what you are writing – get on with putting the words on paper!

You may find that some of your old friends are threatened by the 'new you' and are unsupportive. If this happens, it may be better to end the friendship if it is getting in the way of your writing. Look for people who are going to nurture you and value your emerging talent.

Finally – keep believing in yourself no matter what happens!

Part Seven
Additional Resources

Books for writers

Bingham, H. (2010) The Writer's and Artist's Yearbook Guide to Getting Published

Cameron, J. (1995) The Artist's Way

Cameron, J. (1998) The right to write

Choquette, S. (2011) Your heart's desire: instructions for creating the life you really want

Goldberg, N. (1997) Writing down the bones

Hackles, L. (2008) Writing from life: how to turn your personal experience into profitable prose

Harrold, F. (2001) Indestructible self belief: 7 simple steps to getting it and keeping it

King, S. (2012) On writing: a memoir of the craft

Klauser, H.A. (2001) Write it down, make it happen: knowing what you want and getting it.

Maisel, E. (2008) A writer's space: make room to dream, to work, to write

Malchiodi, C. (2002) The soul's palette: drawing on art's transformative powers for health and well being

Schneider, M and Killick, J. (2009) Writing your self: transforming personal material

Writers and Artists Co. UK (2012) The Writer's and Artist's Yearbook 2013

Writers and Artists Co. UK (2012) Children's Writer's and Artist's Yearbook 2013

Magazines for writers

Aesthetica
(http://www.aestheticamagazine.com/creativewriting)
Mslexia
(http://www.mslexia.co.uk/index.php)
Writer's Forum
(http://www.writers-forum.com/)

Writing Magazine
(https://www.writers-online.co.uk/Writing-Magazine/)
The New Writer
(http://www.thenewwriter.com/)

Websites for writers
Writers and Artists (http://www.writersandartists.co.uk/)
Writer's Digest (http://www.writersdigest.com/)
Writer's Room BBC (http://www.bbc.co.uk/writersroom/)
Writer's Bureau (www.writersbureau.com)

Information on aromatherapy
Websites
Bach Flower Remedies (http://www.bachflower.com/)
Boots website: (www.boots.com) then type 'aromatherapy' into the search bar.
Holland & Barrett website (www.hollandandbarrett.com) then type 'essential oils' or 'aromatherapy' into the search bar.
Books
Schiller, C & Schiller, D. (1994) 500 Formulas for Aromatherapy
Williamson, H. (2011) Aromatherapy Blends and Recipes
Worwood, V.A. (1991) The Complete Book of Essential Oils and Aromatherapy
Worwood, V A (1991) The Fragrant Pharmacy
Worwood, V A (1997) The Fragrant Mind: aromatherapy for personality, mind, mood and emotion

Information on mandalas
Websites
The Mandala Project (http://www.mandalaproject.org)
Google, select 'images' and then type 'free mandala colouring patterns for adults'
Inner Health Studio
(http://www.innerhealthstudio.com/visualization-scripts.html)

Books

Cunningham, L.B. (2010) The Mandala Book: patterns of the universe

Laine, J.E. (2009) Mandala – the art of creating future

Information on mind maps

Websites

Wikipedia: http://en.wikipedia.org/wiki/Mind_map

IQ Matrix: http://iqmatrix.com/

Books

Buzan, T. (2009) The mind map book: unlock your creativity, boost your memory, change your life.

Buzan, T. (2004) Mind maps at work: how to be the best at work and still have time to play.

Buzan, T (2012) The Ultimate Book of Mind Maps

Randall, T.C. (2012) The quick and easy guide to mind map: improve your memory, be more creative and unleash your mind's full potential.

Rustler, F (2012) Mind Mapping for Dummies

Organisations for writers

Arvon (http://www.arvonfoundation.org/)

Crime Writers Association (http://www.thecwa.co.uk/)

Lapidus (http://www.lapidus.org.uk/)

National Association of Memoir Writers (http://www.namw.org/)

Romantic Novelists Association (http://www.rna-uk.org/)

Society of Authors (http://www.societyofauthors.org/)

Society of Children's Book Writer's and Illustrators (http://www.scbwi.org/)

**COMPASS
BOOKS**

Compass Books focuses on practical and informative 'how-to' books for writers. Written by experienced authors who also have extensive experience of tutoring at the most popular creative writing workshops, the books offer an insight into the more specialised niches of the publishing game.